THE 7-DAY SMOOTHIE

Recipe Book

EXPANDED EDITION

50 Delicious Smoothies For Weight Loss

Eric Williams

THE 7 -DAY

PUBLISHED BY:
Eric Williams

ISBN-13: 978-1523931682
ISBN-10: 152393168X

Disclaimer

Disclaimer

The information contained in this ebook is for general information purposes only. The information is provided by the authors and while we endeavor to keep the information up to date and correct, we make no representations or warranties of any kind, express or implied, about the completeness, accuracy, reliability, suitability or availability with respect to the ebook or the information, products, services, or related graphics contained in the ebook for any purpose. Any reliance you place on such information is therefore strictly at your own risk.

Table of Contents

Book Description

There are currently 1.5 billion people worldwide who are overweight according to the Framingham study, and many of those who are normal weight (in particular those who do not exercise) are overweight on this inside. This simply means that their organs are marbled with fat.

The Paleo Diet is the hottest new diet around; because it's the healthiest diet you will ever try. Followers of the diet revert back to the way humans used to eat in the Stone Age when hunter-gathers could only eat what was available to them. Not only will the meats, fish and fresh fruit and vegetables curb your waist line, your health will improve too!

A great asset to the Paleo Diet is the smoothie. It's one of the quickest, most effective ways to fill yourself up without using any empty calories. Here we look at the evidence supporting this, it'll definitely make you think about how you're eating, and what the Paleo lifestyle could do for you!

Chapter 1 - Introduction

The Paleo Diet is the hottest new trend in the food industry, but for a very good reason. It's literally the world's healthiest diet. Originally written about by Loren Cordain, PHD, and based on the theory that the optimal diet for our human bodies is the one that we are genetically adapted to, the theory behind the Paleo Diet is simple. Our hunter-gatherer forefathers, who survived on meat and fish that wasn't combined with growth-stimulating antibiotics or hormones, had it right! The Agriculture Revolution which introduced toxins into the food chain thousands of years ago started the downfall to our diets and subsequently our health. The aim of the Paleo Diet is to get everyone eating as we did way back when, over two million years ago when our diets were dictated by only what was available.

Now the Paleolithic diet is the most researched diet on Google and the diet of choice by many extremely fit and attractive celebrities, such as Ray Mears, Megan Fox and Matthew McConaughey, it's knocked other extremely popular diets off the top spot, including the Atkins Diet, the Dukan Diet and even the Blood Group Diet. The very first all Paleo restaurant has just opened in Colorado, USA called "Blooming Beets" – just a sign of how rapidly this lifestyle is growing. Why is this? There has to be a very good reason that everyone is getting so excited by everything Paleo.

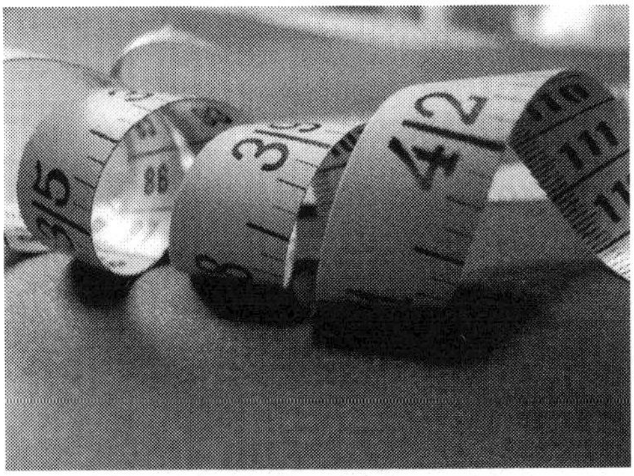

Many scientists believe that the benefits of this diet are tenfold. It's suggested that not only will you lose weight, but you reduce the risk of many modern day inflictions; heart disease, type 2 diabetes and most chronic degenerative diseases. On top of this, it's believed that your athletic performance will improve greatly, making it much easier to introduce activity and exercise into your life – another fantastic aid to weight loss. Combine this with better sleep, increased libido and a clearer mental outlook; you have all the ingredients for a healthier, longer, more active life. Isn't that what everyone really wants?

Many studies have been run to test the effects on the human body, and the results were astounding. The first of these, in 1984 by Dr. Kerin O'Dea, tested diets devoid of grains, dairy and processed foods at the University of Melbourne. Dr O'Dea gathered together 10 middle ages Australian Aborigines. They'd been born in the outback, and had spent their early days primarily as hunter-gatherers until they had been forced to settle into a rural community with access to western goods. All 10 subjects had become overweight and had developed type 2 diabetes as they'd adopted the new lifestyle in their assumed community.

Dr. O'Dae requested that these 10 subjects revert back to their hunter-gatherer lifestyles, the knowledge of which was still ingrained within them, for a seven week period. During this time, they hunted, foraged and gathered. Instead of white bread, sugar and processed foods they switched to birds, fish and bush honey. The results of this were astounding. The average weight loss among the group was 16.5 lbs, their blood cholesterol dropped by 12% and triglycerides were reduced by 72%. On top of that, their insulin and glucose metabolism became normal. Effectively their diabetes disappeared.

The first more recent study happened in 2007. Dr. Lindeberg and associates placed 29 patients with type 2 diabetes and heart disease on either the Paleo Diet or a Mediterranean diet which included the whole grains and low fat dairy products that the Paleo did not. After 12 weeks, the blood glucose toleration levels had improved in both groups, but was noticeably better in the Paleo Dieters.

All the following experiments have shown significant improvement in weight loss, waist size and blood pressure, to name just a few things. This includes the 2009 tests run by Dr. Frasetto and co-workers, where the subjects were put on the Paleo Diet, but their calorie intake remained exactly the same as their previous diet to prove that the improvements were not from calorie reduction, but were in fact from the change in the type of food eaten. The striking thing about these results is that every single participant experienced health improvements.

So now it's obvious why there is such a buzz around the Paleo Diet, but what exactly is it?

Chapter 2 - What is a Paleo Diet?

The Paleo Diet is really quite simple to follow, once you understand the seven basics principles behind it:

- High Protein Intake – Meat, seafood and other animal products make up a staple part of the Paleo Diet. In our current diet, protein only compromises 15% of it, which is considerably lower than the 35% average found in hunter-gatherer diets.

- Lower Carbohydrate Intake – Carbohydrates consume a huge amount of our current diets, but in the Paleo Diet non-starchy fruit and vegetable provide most of what you need. Almost all of these food have low glycemic indices that are slowly absorbed and won't spike your blood sugar levels.

- Higher Fibre Intake – Dietary fibres are essential for good health, but non-starchy fruit and vegetables are actually the best place to find it. Popular belief suggests grains are a good source, but even fruit juices contain twice as much fibres.

- Monounsaturated and Polyunsaturated Fats – It's not the total amount of fat in your diet that can cause numerous health issues, but rather the type of fat. Cut out all of the trans-fat and Omega 6 Polyunsaturated fats in your diet and increase the much healthier Omega 3 and Monounsaturated fats that were staple in Stone Age diets.

- Higher Potassium and Lower Sodium Intake – Unprocessed, fresh foods naturally contain 5 to 10 times more potassium than sodium, and hunter-gatherer bodies were well adapted to this ratio. Low potassium is linked to high blood pressure, heart disease and stroke – the same things problems linked to excessive dietary sodium.

- Net Dietary Alkaline Load that Balances Dietary Acid – After digestion, all food presents a net acid or alkaline load to the kidneys. Meat, fish, grains, legumes and salt produce acid, whereas fruit and vegetables provide alkaline. Too much dietary acid can eventually result in muscle loss, high blood pressure and an increased risk of kidney stones and asthma. An amount of alkaline is needed to balance the acid.

- Higher Intake of Vitamins, Minerals, Antioxidants and Plant Phytochemicals – Whole grains are not a good substitute for grass produced or free ranging meats, fruits and vegetables as they contain no vitamin C, vitamin A or vitamin B12. A lot of the minerals and vitamin B that whole grains do contain are not absorbed well by the body.

So put simply, no grains, no sugar and no processed foods – if the hunter-gatherers from the Stone Age couldn't find it, don't eat it! This seems a very simple premise, but in today's society with so much confusion around food and what's inside it, how do we really know what classes as Paleo?

The list of 'acceptable' meats on the Paleo Diet is very long of course, but you'll want to stay away from anything high in fat or highly processed, such as spam or hot dogs. The same goes for fish, after all fish are full of Omega 3, but many seafood items are also encouraged on the diet; crab, crayfish, crawfish, shrimp, clams, lobster, scallops and oysters.

Almost all vegetables are also 'acceptable', with the exclusion of anything with a high starch value as they tend to be low in nutritional value. This includes potatoes and squashes; the total nutrition is not great in comparison to the amount of starch, carbohydrates and sugar they contain.

Oils and fats are included on the Paleo Diet, contrary to popular belief, as fats don't make you fat – as long as you are eating the right ones! The best types of these, included in the diet are coconut oil, olive oil, macadamia oil, avocado oil and grass fed butter. These natural oils and fats are your bodies preferred way of creating energy, so by including these in your food consumption is simply giving your body what it's asking for.

Nuts are decidedly Paleo (except for peanuts), but if you're trying to lose weight, it's best to watch the amount of nuts you eat because they do contain a lot of fat, in particular cashews.

However, they are a fantastic snack, and extremely tasty.

As we are looking at smoothies here, an extensive list of acceptable fruits is necessary. Of course, most fruits are classed as Paleo, but just to be certain the following are on the 'acceptable' list; apple, avocado, blackberries, papaya, peaches, plum, mango, lychee, blueberries, grapes, lemon, strawberries, watermelon, pineapple guava, lime, raspberries, cantaloupe, tangerine, figs, oranges and bananas. Now while all this fruit is mouth watering, it does contain high fructose levels. While this is much better than high fructose corn syrup, it is still sugar, so it might be best to also have a look at including vegetables in your smoothies if you're main aim is to lose weight.

Whilst looking at what is allowed on the Paleo Diet, you'll also want to know what isn't. This list includes dairy, soft drinks, fruit juices, grains, legumes, artificial sweeteners, fatty meats, salty foods, pre-packaged snacks (such as crisps), starchy vegetables, energy drinks, alcohol and sweets. Cutting out these items might seem daunting, but after all the evidence of the positive effects the diet will have on your life, won't it be worth it in the end?

Here are a few Paleo recipes, just to give you a better idea of the sort of things you can still eat, whilst sticking to this diet that promises to reduce your waist line and improve your health:

Chapter 3 – 7 Delicious Paleo Recipes for Weight Loss

1. **Paleo Jerk Chicken – Serves 3 - 4**
   1-1½ lbs of boneless, skinless chicken thigh
   1 teaspoon of freshly ground black pepper
   ¼ teaspoon of ground turmeric
   ¼ teaspoon of cayenne pepper
   1 teaspoon of ground cumin
   1 teaspoon of dried thyme (or ½ teaspoon of ajwain seeds)
   ¼ teaspoon of garlic powder
   1 teaspoon of bright red paprika
   ½ teaspoon of salt
   3 teaspoons of olive oil

- Preheat the oven to 350F
- Mix the spices together in a small bowl and set aside
- Cut the chicken thighs into 1 inch segments and place in a separate bowl
- Add the spice mix plus 1 teaspoon of olive oil to the chicken, mix well and set aside for 10 minutes
- Heat the remaining olive oil in a wok or non stick frying pan over a very high heat, when the oil is very hot, add the chicken
- Stir fry quickly until the pieces are lightly browned or have turned opaque on the outside
- Place the chicken pieces into a baking dish and cover loosely with lightly oiled wax paper (which should sit inside the dish and directly on top of the chicken pieces) and bake for 8 – 10 minutes or until the chicken is cooked
- Enjoy whilst hot, or remove from the hot baking dish to retain the moisture for later

2. **Calamari Salad – Serves 4**
   1 lb wild caught sliced squid tentacles – pre-cooked
   ½ cup of extra virgin olive oil
   1 teaspoon of white vinegar
   ¼ teaspoon of white pepper
   1 sliced red or yellow pepper
   4 cups of mixed green lettuce
   1 bunch of cilantro leaves
   10 low sodium olives rinsed and sliced
   1 sliced red onion
   2 large tomatoes

- Combine the calamari with the olive oil, the teaspoon of white vinegar and sliced pepper then set aside
- Toss together the mixed greens and cilantro and spread evenly on a large serving platter
- Add remaining ingredients to the lettuce mixture
- When you're ready to eat, scoop squid mixture onto greens and toss together

3. **Raw Chocolate Covered Walnuts with Berries – Serves 3 - 4**
   One 3.5 oz bar of raw dark chocolate (at least 85%, but 99% if possible)
   20 raw sprouted organic walnut halves
   12 large organic fresh strawberries

- Place chocolate in a double boiler pot on top of a lower pot filled with water
- Bring water to a simmer and stir chocolate with a wooden spoon until melted
- Remove chocolate from heat
- Using a fork, dip one berry into the chocolate at a time and place on wax paper to cool
- Do the same with the walnut halves
- Dust with nutmeg, cinnamon, or cayenne if desired
- If not eating immediately, keep in a tightly sealed plastic container for no longer than a week.

4. **Paleo Zucchini Bread – Serves 3 - 4**
   ¾ cup coconut flour
   1 cup grated zucchini or 1 small zucchini
   1 ripe banana, mashed
   10 pitted dates (soaked in water for 30 minutes)
   3 tablespoon ground flaxseeds + 9 tablespoon water
   1 teaspoon of baking powder
   1 teaspoon of cinnamon
   ½ teaspoon of sea salt

- Preheat oven to 350°F.
- Add the 3 tablespoon flaxseeds and 9 tablespoon water to a bowl and mix thoroughly. Place

in the fridge.

- In a large bowl, mix the coconut flour, baking powder, cinnamon and salt.
- Drain and rinse the dates, then add to a blender along with a little water. You might need to use up to 1 cup of water, but just add a bit at a time until the mix becomes a caramel consistency, similar to this Date Paste.
- Once the dates have formed a thick caramel, add to the large bowl along with the zucchini and mashed banana.
- Remove the flaxseed and water mix from the fridge and add to the bowl.
- Mix all ingredients thoroughly together.
- Line a small loaf tin with baking paper.
- Spoon the bread batter evenly into the loaf tin. Smooth down the top of the bread with the spoon.
- Bake for about 20 to 35 minutes depending on your type of oven. The bread should be lightly golden on top and soft to the touch. Place a skewer in the center. If it comes out clean, it's ready!
- Remove from the oven, place on a wire rack and leave to cool for 10 minutes.
- Once the tin has cooled, gently lift the bread out in the baking paper.
- Slice and enjoy!

5. **One-pot fish with black olives & tomatoes – Serves 4**

175g black olives in oil, stones removed
1 large onion, roughly chopped
400g can chopped tomatoes
4 boneless white fish fillets such as Icelandic cod or hoki, each weighing about 175g/6oz

- Place chocolate in a double boiler pot on top of a lower pot filled with water
- Preheat the oven to fan 180C/conventional 200C/gas 6.
- Heat 1 tablespoon of the oil from the olives in an ovenproof pan.
- Tip in the onion and stir well, leave to cook for a minute or two and then give it another good stir.
- Add the tomatoes and some salt and pepper.
- Bring to the boil, then add the olives.
- Put the fish, skin side down, onto the sauce and drizzle over a splash more oil from the olive jar.
- Bake, uncovered, for 15 minutes until the fish is cooked.
- Sprinkle with chopped parsley and serve straight from the pan, with lemon wedges for squeezing over.

6. **Ahi Tuna with Angel Hair Pasta – Serves 4**

1 Pound angel hair pasta
1 small shallot, diced
1 zucchini, chopped
1/2 Cup red bell pepper, thinly sliced
1/2 Cup mini-roma tomatoes, cut in half (or cherry tomatoes)
3 Tablespoons champagne vinegar

1/4 Cup olive oil, divided
1/4 Cup reserved pasta water
Fresh cilantro
1 Tablespoon Spanish paprika
2 Teaspoons ground coriander
1 Teaspoon dried oregano
1 Teaspoon chili power
1 1/2 Teaspoon ground mustard
Olive oil for searing
Four 4-ounce fillets of ahi tuna

- Cook the pasta by following the package less 2 minutes and set aside in a bowl. You can add a little water or olive oil while it sits. Reserve 1 cup of pasta water.
- Take a large sauté pan over medium heat and add in 1 tablespoon olive oil. Add in shallot and cook for 2 minutes. Next add in zucchini and bell pepper. Let sauté for 4 minutes. Turn heat off and add in tomatoes and champagne vinegar. Let sit until tuna is ready.
- In a small bowl combine paprika, coriander, oregano, chili powder, and ground mustard. Move to a plate and coat each tuna on both sides. Set a side.
- Heat your indoor grill pan over medium-high heat. Once hot add in olive oil to coat the bottom of the pan. Add tuna and sear for 2-3 minutes (depending on the thickness). Flip over and turn off heat and let the fish heat through.
- Take the pan with the vegetables and turn to medium heat. Once hot add in pasta, 2 tablespoons olive oil and using thongs to combine ingredients. Add in cilantro and if you need more liquid add some pasta water 1 tablespoon at a time. Taste for any additional seasonings.
- On a board slice tuna.
- To serve add pasta to the bottom of the plate and divide the tuna pieces to 4 plates.

7. **Chicken Vegetable Soup – Serves 3 - 4**

Fat of Choice {I used Coconut Oil}
1 medium onion, medium dice
3 medium carrots, medium dice
1 zucchini, medium dice
¼ medium butternut squash, chopped into cubes
12 oz. container of mushrooms, rough dice
2-4 cups shredded chicken
1 teaspoon dried thyme
1-2 teaspoon dried rosemary + dried basil
½-1 teaspoon ground cumin
1 tablespoon Apple Cider Vinegar
salt + pepper
around half a batch of chicken stock
Lemon {optional}

- Get a big soup pot on the stove heating on medium with your favorite fat -- I liked coconut oil here because it really warmed up the soup's flavor!
- Clean + chop your vegetables and add them in -- literally this is a chop + drop soup. Meaning as you chop just drop it all in and stir occasionally.

- Add in as much chicken as you want, I did somewhere between 3-4 cups. I like a lot of chicken in my soup!
- Add in your herbs, cumin, apple cider vinegar, salt + pepper and stir everything together well.
- Add in your chicken stock -- I used around half of a batch but honestly just use as much as you want. You want it to cover the vegetables and chicken but after that it's totally up to you how much you add in. And if you don't have enough stock on hand you can always add in a little bit of water!
- Stir everything up, cover {with the lid cracked just a little}, and let simmer on low for around an hour or until dinner!
- When serving I like to squeeze on a little bit of fresh lemon juice! It makes it even more yummy that it already is!

So as these example recipes demonstrate, the possibilities on the Paleo Diet are endless – you can even allow yourself a little treat now and again, provided you tread carefully. Smoothies are another snack that can help you along the way, and that is what the next section will look at in more detail.

Chapter 4 - Why Smoothie Recipes Really Work?

A smoothie is a blended beverage made from fresh fruit and vegetables. Smoothies are a fantastic way to help you lose weight, particularly on the Paleo Diet as you have full control of what you're putting into your body. You control the ingredients, and even though they are very healthy, they also hold the power to keep you full for a long period of time, which is an ideal aid to weight loss. Everything that goes into that glass is your choice, which means there are no empty or added calories, and if that isn't enough, smoothies can also help boost your metabolic rate which leaves you with much more energy.

Smoothie diets are another thing that has become very popular in recent years, but advocates of the Paleo Diet suggest introducing smoothies into your regular diet, as a snack or for breakfast. Consuming only smoothies is often only a 'quick fix' and the Paleo Diet looks for long term results. It's more of a lifestyle change. This aside, they are a fantastic and delicious way to get the fruit and vegetable ingredients necessary in the Paleo Diet. Smoothies containing a lot of vegetables are often referred to as 'Green Smoothies'.

There is a lot of evidence to support the fact that smoothies support weight loss and are a great way to consume your fruit and vegetables. The main point of this argument is that smoothies take out the necessity to chew our food. All plants are composed of cells which contain a lot of cellulose, which is a type of carbohydrate. Human do not have the enzyme needed to break down cellulose which means we can't use it as the energy source it's designed to be. The only way we can gain all of the necessary nutrients, is by chewing our food thoroughly.

However, this is rarely done and up to 90% of cells are not open, and the nutrients aren't released. A way to overcome this is by using the blending process. This ensures a much higher number of nutrients will be absorbed into your bloodstream. On top of that, heat softens the cellulose walls of vegetables, which also aids absorption.

All of this information suggests that if you're considering trying the Paleo Diet (and I'm sure you are by now!) then smoothies are an amazing addition that you'll really want to try. Below are some Paleo Diet smoothie recipes, just to get you started.

Chapter 5 - 50 Delicious Smoothie Recipes for Weight Loss

All ingredients in these recipes must be mixed together in a blender or food processor until well incorporated.

1. **Key Lime Pie Green Smoothie.**

   2 tablespoon of key lime juice (about 4 limes)
   1 teaspoon of key lime zest (about 2 limes)
   1 cup of unsweetened non-dairy milk
   1 ripe frozen banana
   ¼ teaspoon of alcohol-free vanilla extract
   2 drops of liquid stevia or 1 tablespoon of ground xylitol or 1 pitted medjool date
   1 tablespoon of sunflower butter
   2 cups of organic baby spinach
   4 ice cubes
   1 minute vanilla whipped topping (optional)
   gluten-free graham cracker pieces (optional)

2. **Apple Cinnamon Pie Smoothie.**
   1 cup of chopped, peeled apples
   1 tablespoon of honey
   1 teaspoon of cinnamon powder
   ½ teaspoon of vanilla essence
   ¼ cup of unsalted cashew nuts
   1 cup of coconut milk

3. **Blueberry Acai Smoothie**

1 cup coconut milk
1 ½ frozen bananas
1 cup frozen blueberries
1 cup frozen strawberries
1 cup acai juice
¾ cup ice

4. **Almost Pina Colada Smoothie**
1 cup of pineapple juice, fresh or with no added sugar
1 cup of coconut milk
½ lime (juice only)
1 banana
A few cubes of ice

5. **Emerald Kale & Mango Smoothie**
1 mango, peeled, diced, stone removed
2 cups f fresh kale - 2 branches, stem removed, leaves torn and washed
½ lime, juice only
1 kiwifruit, peeled and diced
1 cup of cold coconut milk

6. **Strawberry Coconut Almond Smoothie**
8-10 small frozen strawberries
3 fresh strawberries
250ml of coconut milk
1 teaspoon of almond butter
1 teaspoon of honey

7. **Mixed Berry & Chocolate Paleo Smoothie**
1 cup of frozen mixed berries
250ml of coconut milk
2 tablespoons of gluten-free jam
A few dark chocolate shavings.

8. **Banana Date Smoothie**
2 frozen bananas, sliced
4 small dates
1 tablespoon of smooth peanut butter
1 tablespoon of chia seeds
½ cup of hemp milk
¼ cup of water

9. **Many Berry Smoothie**
4-5 ice cubes

½ cup of water
1 cup of strawberries
½ cup of blueberries
1 mashed banana

10. **Spinach Banana Smoothie**
2 oranges, juice only
½ lemon, juice only
1 cup of spinach
1 cup of kale
1 banana
A handful of fresh mint and coriander

11. **Coconut Surprise Smoothie**
½ cup of coconut water
1 cup of pineapple chunks
¾ of a banana
A handful of ice

12. **Orange Nutmeg Smoothie**
2 grated carrots
2 peeled oranges
½ cup of water
Pinch of nutmeg

13. **Peach Zing Smoothie**
3 peaches
¾ mashed banana
1 teaspoon of grated ginger
½ a cup of water
A handful of icecubes

14. **Superberry Smoothie**
4-5 ice cubes
½ a cup of water
1 cup of strawberries
½ a cup of raspberries
½ a cup of blackberries
1 cup of blueberries

15. **Kale and Berry Smoothie**
1 cup of kale
1 cup of strawberries

½ a cup of blueberries
¾ mashed banana
½ cup of water

16. Apricot soy smoothie

1 cup no-added-sugar pie fruit apricot halves
2 x 175g tubs apricot and mango low-fat soy yoghurt
½ cup calcium-enriched reduced-fat soy milk
8 ice cubes

17. Grape Banana Smoothie

1 small banana
1 cup seedless red grapes
1 cup Vanilla Lowfat Yogurt
1 cup Grape Juice
1 pinch ground cinnamon

18. Peach and honey smoothie

410g can peach slices in juice, drained
¾ cup reduced-fat vanilla yoghurt
2 teaspoons honey
1 cup reduced-fat milk

19. Tropical Bump Smoothie

1 banana, peeled
½ cup frozen diced mango
½ cup frozen diced pineapple
1 cup light coconut milk
1 tablespoon lime juice
4 ice cubes
Toasted coconut flakes

20. Melon Ginger Smoothie

1 cup chopped honeydew melon
½ cup chopped peeled kiwi
½ ripe banana, sliced
¼ cup white grape juice
½ teaspoon ginger juice
2 teaspoons lime juice
½ cup lemon sorbet
½ cup ice

21. **Avocado Green Smoothie**

1 cup filtered water
½ avocado (peeled/pitted)
½ green apple
1 banana (peeled)
1 orange (peeled)
1 lemon (peeled)
½ lime (peeled)
1 big bunch parsley
4 ice cubes

22. **Orange Creamsicle Smoothie**

1 orange, peeled and seeds removed
¼ cup fat-free vanilla yogurt
2 tablespoons frozen orange juice concentrate
¼ teaspoon vanilla extract
4 ice cubes

23. **Pear and Greens Smoothie**

1 pear
1 banana
2 celery sticks
1 cup water
1 bunch of Italian parsley
½ cucumber

24. **Mango Coconut Green Smoothie**

½ cup coconut water
¾ cup low-fat cottage cheese
1 cup chopped kale
1 cup frozen banana slices
½ cup frozen mango
1 tablespoon flaxseed or flaxmeal
1-2 teaspoons pure maple syrup or honey

25. **Kiwi and coconut quinoa smoothie**

½ cup Jalna Coconut Yoghourt
1 teaspoon grated ginger
2 kiwifruit, peeled
2 tablespoons quinoa flakes
10g baby spinach

26. Fruity Dandelion Greens Smoothie

½ ripe peach
½ mango
¼ cup apple
1 cup dandelion greens
¼ cup water

27. Citrus Berry Smoothie

1¼ cups fresh berries
¾ cup low-fat plain yogurt
½ cup orange juice
2 tablespoons nonfat dry milk
1 tablespoon toasted wheat germ
1 tablespoon honey
½ teaspoon vanilla extract

28. Papaya Smoothie

2 cups chopped peeled seeded papayas
1 cup chilled pineapple juice
½ cup milk
½ cup sliced banana
1 tablespoon honey
2 teaspoons fresh lime juice
4 ice cubes

29. Apple Milk Smoothie

2 red apples
2 tablespoons sugar
2 teaspoons rose water or 2 teaspoons orange flower water
2 cups cold milk
4 ice cubes

30. Cranberry Orange Smoothie

700ml water
½ cup frozen cranberries
2 oranges, peeled
4 tablespoons walnuts
2 tablespoons honey
1 teaspoon vanilla extract
8 ice cubes

31. Banana Agave Smoothie

1 cup plain fat-free yogurt

½ cup fresh or frozen blueberries, thawed
2 teaspoons light-colored agave nectar
1 chilled sliced ripe banana

32. **Blueberry Oatmeal Smoothie**
1 cup unsweetened almond milk
½ banana
¼ cup rolled oats
2 tablespoons raw almonds
½ teaspoons stevia
1 cup frozen blueberries

33. **Avocado Smoothie**
1 ripe avocado
2 cups sweetened almond milk
1 cup crushed ice
¼ cup fat-free sweetened condensed milk
2 tablespoons fresh lime juice
1 tablespoon chopped slivered almonds, toasted

34. **Parsley Passion Green Smoothie**
1½ cups water
1 cup pineapple chunks
½ cucumber
1 banana
¼ bunch of parsley
4 ice cubes

35. **Strawberry Mango Spring Smoothie**
1 cup coconut milk
1 banana, peeled, sliced, and frozen
1 mango, skinned and chunked
5 large strawberries, hulled

36. **Chocolate-Banana Sipper Smoothie**
2 cups fat-free milk
1 banana, sliced and frozen
3 tablespoons unsweetened cocoa powder
2 tablespoons honey
1 teaspoon vanilla

37. **Carrot Mango Green Tea Smoothie**
3 cups water
1 cup sliced carrots or packaged peeled baby carrots
1 inch fresh ginger, thinly sliced

4 green tea bags
2 cups frozen mango chunks
1 teaspoon honey
1 tablespoon chia seeds

38. Banana Yoghurt Granola Smoothie

1 Banana
1 cup Granola
2 cups Vanilla Yoghurt
5 Almonds

39. Lime Refresher smoothie

1 Banana
2 Limes, peeled
200 ml Apple juice
1 teaspoon Ginger, grated

40. Apple Ginger Smoothie

1 chopped peeled apple
1½-inch piece peeled ginger,
the juice of 2 limes,
¼ cup honey
1 cup water and 2 cups ice.

41. Pomegranate-Berry Smoothie

1 cup blueberries,
¾ cup each beet juice and pomegranate juice
1 cup ice, and honey to taste.

42. Mamey and chia seed smoothie

1 cup mamey (sapote) ripe, seeded and cut into chunks
½ cup of fresh almond milk
1 tablespoon of honey (optional)
1½ tablespoon of chia seeds
1 pinch of salt (optional)
4 ice cubes

43. Strawberry Banana Smoothie

1 cup strawberries,
½ cup each vanilla yogurt and milk
2 teaspoons honey

a pinch of cinnamon and 1 cup ice.

44. **Almond Orange Smoothie**
1 cup vanilla-flavoured almond beverage
½ cup orange juice
1 lemon Juice
1 lime Juice
4 ice cubes
1 tablespoon honey

45. **Blackberry Yogurt Smoothie**
1 cup yoghurt
3 cups blackberries
1 cup buttermilk
3 tablespoons honey
pinch ground cardamom

46. **Triple Berry Ginger Smoothie**
½ Cup of Frozen Blueberries
½ Cup of Frozen Strawberries
½ Cup of Frozen Blackberries
½ tablespoon of Fresh Ginger
½ Cup Soy Milk

47. **Strawberry Cocoa Smoothie**
1½ cup Unsweetened Coconut Milk
½ cup Water
1 cup Ice
2 tablespoon Honey
4 tablespoon Almond Butter
4 tablespoon Cocoa
2 Bananas
20 Strawberries

48. **Mango lychee and yoghurt smoothie**
2 cups Milk
¾ Natural yoghurt
1 Banana
1 tablespoon Honey
½ cup Mango, fresh, diced
8 Lychees, tinned

49. Frozen Fruit Smoothie

2 cups of orange juice
1 cup of frozen berries
1 banana
1 tablespoon chia seeds
3 tablespoon rolled oats

50. Veggie Smoothie

6 sticks of celery
300ml organic apple juice
2cm fresh ginger
1 cucumber
500g Glenisk Organic Natural Yogurt
1 tablespoon of honey

When blended, all these recipes create a unique tasting, Paleo Diet smoothie which won't only aid your weight loss mission, but also taste fantastic too! The possibilities for creating your own Paleo Diet Smoothies are endless, so why not give it a try?

Resources

www.happyhealthylonglife.com

www.thepaleodiet.com

www.paleoleap.com

www.paleorecipebook.com

www.eatdrinkpaleo.com

www.webmd.com

www.morguefile.com

www.dummies.com

THANK YOU
FOR
READING

~ If You Enjoyed Reading This Book Please Leave A Review On Amazon ~

Preview of 'The 7-Day Weight Loss Motivation'

Book Description

The whole report is about how to motivate you towards weight loss. After going through it you will find yourself into another world which is attractive and smart world for you and that is your world. Because you are smart and slim than before with best figure just because of weight loss. Some of the success stories are also included in it to motivate you to get ready for your weight loss. Don't be afraid it's as easy as you want. This report has solution for your problems of obesity, fat belly and weight. Once you start reading it you can't leave it without its complete study. it will catch your attraction because it have everything in it diet, tips, stories and the most weight loss friendly foods. it will increase your information and decrease your tension.

The world of achievement has always belonged to the optimist. (J. Harold Wilkins)

So never lose a hope that you can't do anything or you don't have solution regarding your weight. Here is your solution in this report there is solution for your all problems regarding weight loss. It will boost your confidence that you can lose your weight. This report will increase your motivation. Motivation is the most important factor because without motivation you can't get required results and I must said this report is the motivational report so must read it and change your life and enjoy it in a beautiful way. Looks adorable is everyone's wish and that will come true by reading this report.

Chapter 1 - Motivation and Motivational Quotes

This chapter provide basic information about motivation and to elaborate the motivation there are some motivational quotes to motivate you towards weight loss.

Motivation and Motivational Quotes

- Believe in you
- No more excuses
- No pain no gain
- Take first step today
- Love your body
- Work for it

Objectives

Make you motivated towards weight loss with the help of quotes and gives you some suggestion that how to do that.

Motivation and Motivational Quotes

Little by little does the trick. (Aesop).

Motivation is something which pushes you to take a start. Without motivation you can't get the desired results. Because only motivation can takes you towards your destiny. And when it comes to motivation of weight loss one can't get the desired results without motivation even you follow the perfect diet plan. Below are the some motivational quotes which will definitely motivate towards weight loss.

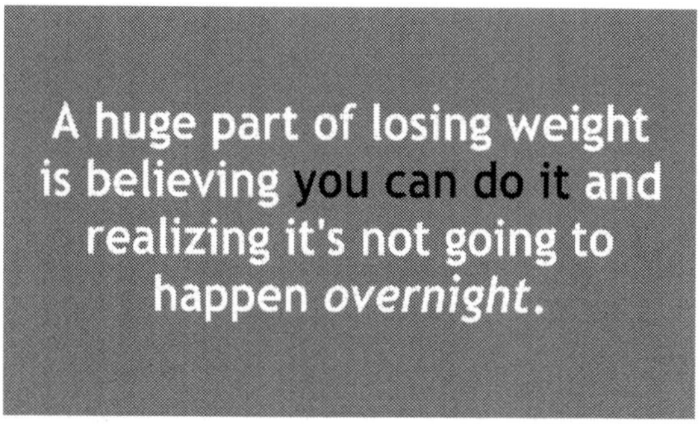

Self confidence and weight loss are interconnected with each other. Because believing in yourself is the key to any success and when it comes to weight loss it raises your self confidence because of your achievement. Patience and believing in your self is the two main factors which have be with you because weight loss will not happen in seconds or in day or two. So keep patience and walk on your way.

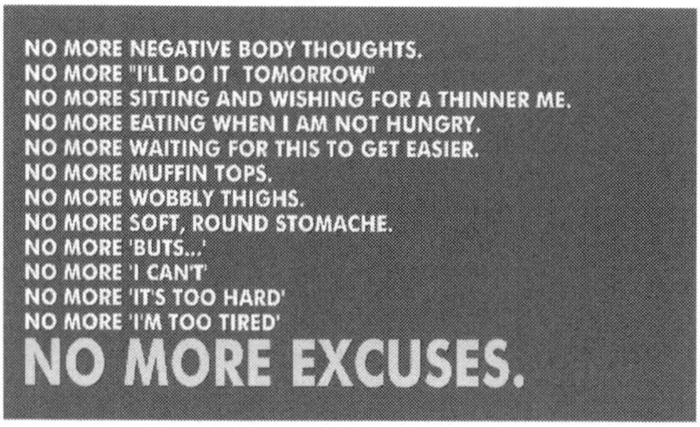

Don't give any excuse to yourself. Because by giving excuse to yourself will never let you to achieve your task. Excuses are given by the loser and believe in yourself that you are not a loser you are the winner this will motivate you towards your destiny. Think about different opportunities which you will get after weight loss and that will motivate you towards weight loss.

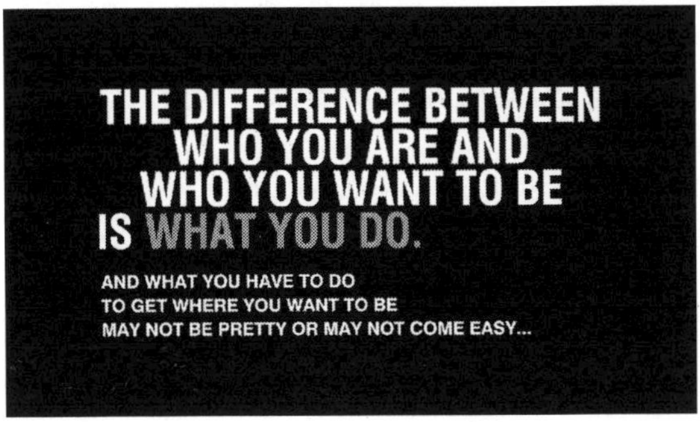

Every person has a dream what he/she wanted to be and that one can get by only doing something regarding that dream. So when it comes to weight loss try to get your dream comes true and that will only happens when you try for it. So don't wait and get started today and you will get it one day believe in this. Because as it is said that slow and steady win the race. So never lose your hope tomorrow will be yours.

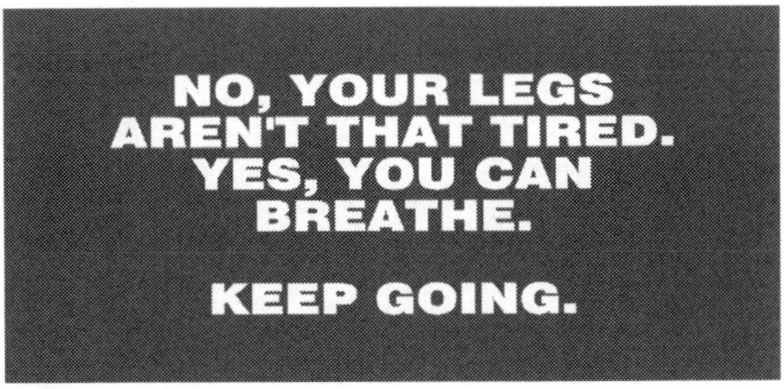

Bearing pain is another important factor while you motivate yourself towards weight loss. Because only brave persons can conquers the world. And it's time to conquer your dreams so never lose hopes by the ups and downs they will take you towards your dream world.

Challenge yourself on daily basis. That will change your mood, hope and increase your patience. Challenge will be a gigantic step towards healthier lifestyle. Take your weight loss as a challenge for yourself and accept that challenge whole heartedly and try to beat that challenge will make you the winner.

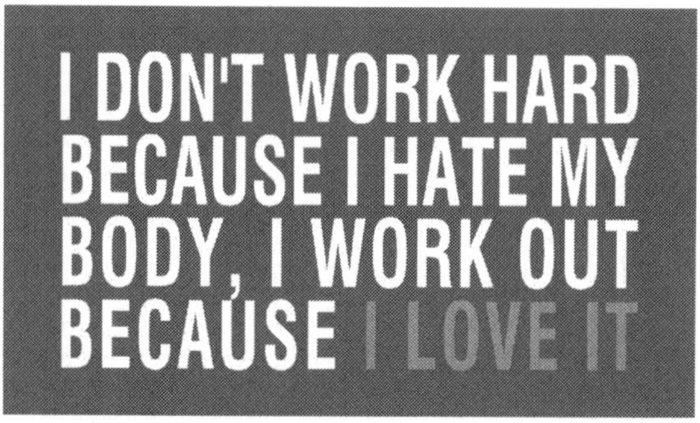

If you are fluffy don't hate your body. Love your body in any condition or in any situation. Because love can change anything and love has the power to make impossible things become possible. When you love your body you will try to make it beautiful. And try to work on it and improve it to the extent that it will be loved by everyone.

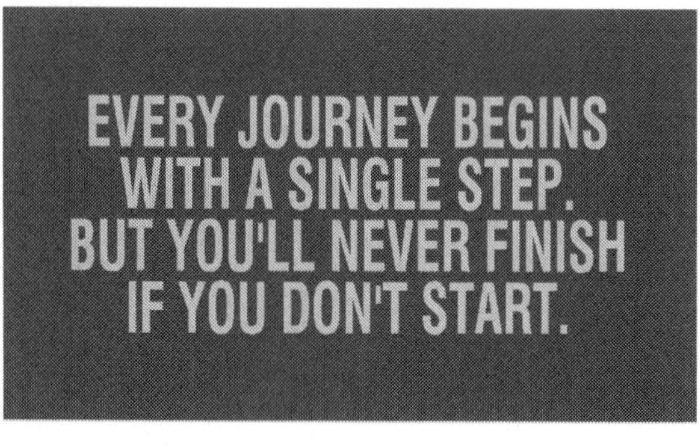

Pythagoras said: "the beginning is half the whole". So get start from today because only first step is difficult when you get started it becomes easier for you. Because you can only finish when you get started so take a start don't hesitate it's easy and you can do it.

Magic's doesn't exist in real world. Wish can't come true by magic. You have to work for it then your wish becomes true otherwise wish will remain a wish it will never come true.

Tell it to yourself or decide it by yourself that are you a weight loss winner or weight loss loser. Losers give excuse and find the way to escape and winners find the way to get it done. So find the way and get started. Let put the defeat beneath your feet's and walk on it towards your goal and make your own success story.

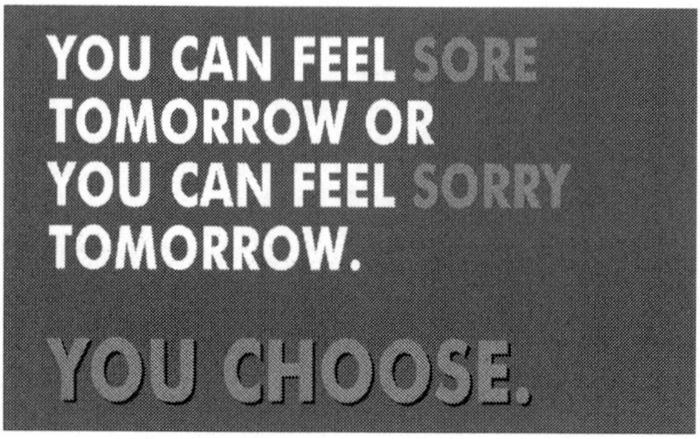

Feelings are very important to every person. The feelings which you want are in your hands. You want to have happy feeling or sad. That is in your hand that you make your tomorrow happy or sad. Achievement or disappointment is in your hand work for it and get it.

Chapter 2 - Think Yourself Slim

Attitude makes huge difference in our life. So this chapter describe how to change your attitude if you want to lose weight because it's not only the physical game it's mental game also and it will be elaborated through this chapter.

- Motivation
- Choose goal
- Make plan
- Visualization
- Change your thought
- Make your priorities
- Celebrate

Objective

To change your attitude

Think Yourself Slim

Attitude makes the difference. So change your attitude towards yourself and it will make the difference. Following are the eight simple tricks which will motivate you towards weight loss. So keep them in view they will really help you out.

Define Your Motivation:-

Weight loss is something about burning calories and makes you slim. But your mental viewpoint is very important here you have to believe that it will never happen overnight. Thinks that it is a long term project will turn it in a challenge for you and you have to take that challenge. In your mind you have a lot of reasons of weight loss. But pick up the one which is the most stronger. Don't put your reasons like I have to change them in a way that I want do that will really make the difference because a person can do any sort of work for his/her own wish and will instead of some duty. So make it your wish it will really work for you.

Amazon 2 5-17-16

31888474R00020

Made in the USA
Middletown, DE
15 May 2016